Making Room for the Light

Kristie E. Jackson

Unless otherwise indicated, all Scriptures are from the ESV® Bible
(The Holy Bible, English Standard Version®) copyright © 2001 by Crossway
Bibles, a publishing ministry of Good News Publishers. ESV® Text Edition: 2007.
The ESV® text has been reproduced in cooperation with and
by permission of Good News Publishers.

Copyright © 2014 Kristie E. Jackson

All rights reserved.

ISBN-13: 978-1503336834

For Dub, Nate and Sam

INTRODUCTION

In early December of 2013, I had occasion to see one of my beloved former babysitters. This lovely twenty-something, Lauren, gave up caring for my sons and instead got married and had a family of her own.

We had lunch on Lauren's deck on an unseasonably warm day when her daughter, Kate, was also home. I believe an inquisitive, easily-delighted two-year-old is about the best companion there is. Kate was a lovely lunch date, and her eyes danced with excitement over every little thing.

She was all smiles until I was given a tour of the house and we came to the mantel over the fireplace. Upon the mantel was a Nativity scene. She pointed with her usual enthusiasm at "lamby" and a goat. But when we came to Mary and Joseph, she shook her darling little head, the wispy curls around her ears bobbing with emphasis, "No room," she said, with a sort of stunned wonder, "No room."

Somehow this little one knew this was very profound. Mary and Joseph were turned away from the inn because there was no room for them.

I've been pondering these two simple words, "no room," and have come to believe that it wasn't just Mary and Joseph's Christmas crisis, it's ours as well. We have no room for welcoming and celebrating the birth of Our Savior. No room.

We get caught up in the perfunctory festivities, trying to meet or exceed grandiose expectations fueled mostly by savvy marketing. Our calendars may be jammed with parties and events, but peace and joy are often fleeting.

We are left with no room emotionally, physically or spiritually to unwrap and celebrate the best gift that was ever given. Thus, the aim of these Advent readings is very simple: to make room for contemplating and rejoicing over the birth of Jesus, the Light of the world.

May this season be less hurried, more peace and joy-filled than any you can remember. Over the next twenty-four days may you make room for the Light, and rejoice daily over His birth.

Joy to the world! the Lord is come; Let earth receive her King.
Let every heart prepare Him room.

May every heart "prepare Him room."

DECEMBER 1
PROACTIVE PONDERING

We have a much-treasured wooden Advent calendar, which a dear friend gave me when my eldest son, Will, was just two and my son, Nate, was a newborn. Christmas in our home wouldn't be Christmas without this beautiful calendar being prominently displayed and opened each day leading up to December 25th.

In 2013 when our third and youngest son, Sam, was six, he woke up early on December 1st and said, "Let's go downstairs and do our math thing." Neither Will nor Nate ever talked about the Advent calendar having anything to do with math, but this child is his own man. So we went down and he pulled out the number one door, unwrapped the little star magnet and hung it over the painted image of the manger. I love the anticipation this simple ritual builds. As Sam reasoned, "we all know Jesus is behind the 24." Yet that doesn't diminish the fun of unwrapping the story every day.

As we approach December 25th and celebrate the most important, world-altering Gift ever given, I try to be intentional with my family, talking and thinking through what we are celebrating. Music, decorations and special events are embraced in our home, but I aim to make these outward signs merely symbolic of inward reflections. I've done this with varying degrees of success over the years. Never have I reached Christmas and thought, "Boy, we nailed it this year!" Instead, I always wish we'd spent more time being quiet and contemplative, more time serving, more time praying. I do know that daily readings have helped me in my efforts to focus, and writing for me is a discipline as well. I identify with Marilynne Robinson's narrator in *Gilead*, who said, "For me writing has always felt like praying, even when I wasn't writing prayers."[1]

But whether you read or write, listen to music or pray -- perhaps you'll combine all of these -- it matters less what your plan is, and more that you have *a* plan. If we aren't intentional, our days will slip by without time for reflection. It's possible for every moment of our days to be filled -- your life might be marked by amazing productivity, or you may be more apt to spend too much time passively sitting in front of a screen. Living in the 21st Century means that we can very easily fill every spare second. For heaven's sake, we check our smart phones when we are standing in line, mindlessly choosing to absorb more information via these handheld devices. But maybe this gap-filling -- this implicit yet habitual rejection of white space -- is itself a vice. Maybe it robs us of the full and contemplative lives we were designed for. When Jesus said he wanted us to have a full and abundant life, He didn't mean for us to never have a spare moment. Instead He modeled taking time away, to think and to pray. This Advent

---

[1] Marilynne Robinson, *Gilead* (New York: Picador, 2004), 19.

season – this time of anticipating the birth of Jesus – may we consistently carve out white space.

Perhaps you can decide today where and when you will spend time reflecting over the next three and a half weeks. You may want to light a candle or play classical Christmas music or be able to see the lights on your tree. But make a commitment to creating a lovely space to slowly and methodically unwrap the gift of Jesus' birth.

Each reading will include Scripture, questions for reflection, and a closing prayer. It is my hope and prayer that this little book will be a blessing to you this season.

Recommended Scripture

Psalm 111

Questions for Reflection

What is your favorite Christmas memory from your childhood? What made it special? What made other Christmas memories less than fulfilling? Was it unmet expectations? Did those memories lack deeper meaning?

Closing Prayer

Heavenly Father, may this Christmas season be about celebrating Your Son. May rejoicing over His birth be the focus of my heart more this year than ever. May all the festivities be outward manifestations of inner praise. Help me, Lord, to be intentional in the days ahead, to have a grateful and compassionate heart today and everyday. In Jesus' Name, Amen.

DECEMBER 2
THE HUMILITY OF CHRIST

Have you ever really stopped to consider that the earthly life of the King of Kings and Lord of Lords was marked by humility? In fact, the life of Jesus was bookended by incredibly humble situations: being born in a lowly stable and being hung on the cross as a criminal. Act One of Jesus' life opens in a barn, because no one had room for Him and His family. The Final Act begins in the Upper Room, where He is washing the dirty feet of His friends. From there, He suffers first the betrayal by Judas, then the discouraging inability of His very closest friends to support Him in His darkest hour (remember they kept falling asleep), then He endures mocking and barbaric physical abuse, and is ultimately crucified. Can we really get our heads around what He gave up to do this?

Our culture, our leaders, our VIPs daily exhibit the antithesis of the mindset of Christ. Americans are so much about glory, about comfort, about getting what we deserve. Seldom do we hear about anyone foregoing anything they're entitled to. We may hear about a CEO or a professional athlete working in a soup kitchen, but even that sometimes seems undertaken with an eye to public relations. "Servant leadership" is a term bandied about, but few of us can point to many real-life examples.

But Jesus gave up Heaven! Heaven, as in better than we can even imagine! To be born in a stable. To be a helpless Babe not raised in the courts of privilege, but in an ordinary family with ordinary jobs and zero glory. And Mary was not the kind of girl who would've posted selfies with the Christ Child. No, she was quiet, pondering it all in her heart. Joseph carried on with life as a carpenter. He didn't try to capitalize on the smarts of his Son – at least we don't have any record of Joseph trying to somehow showcase that Jesus was the smartest person anyone had ever met, like we'd see on some reality show today.

Instead Jesus never demanded his due. He exuded gentleness, a quiet peace. He was unassuming and unpretentious. He exemplified humility from beginning to end.

This season, may we too be willing to adopt a posture of humility. C.S. Lewis said, "If anyone would like to acquire humility, I can, I think, tell him the first step; the first step is to realise that one is proud. And a biggish step, too. At least, nothing whatever can be done before it. If you think you are not conceited, it means you are very conceited indeed."[2]

Recommended Scripture

James 4

Questions for Reflection

Who in your life is truly humble? Truly willing to serve others without reward? Is it hard to do nice things without being acknowledged? How

---

[2] C.S. Lewis, *Mere Christianity* (New York: Simon & Schuster, 1943), 114.

can we do something in the next few weeks that is thoughtful and anonymous?

Closing Prayer

Heavenly Father, I know that I am not like Jesus. I am proud. I don't want to forego what I "deserve." I want recognition. I don't want to be humbled and embarrassed and mistreated. Help me to understand that part of knowing Jesus and reflecting Jesus is emulating His humility. Forgive me. Help me to grow in all dimensions of Christlikeness, but most especially today, help me to be humble, to be ever-willing to sacrifice my own agenda for Yours. In Jesus' Name, Amen.

DECEMBER 3
BRIDLING BITTERNESS

Have you ever been turned away in an hour of need? Surely Mary and Joseph must have wondered why on earth God couldn't have arranged for a last minute cancellation at the inn. Imagine how physically exhausted they must have been. We think long car trips are taxing. We think long flights are draining. We can hardly fathom making the kind of 70 or 80 mile trek Mary and Joseph made either on foot or on the back of a donkey while very pregnant. I can vividly picture my own husband's reaction if we were then turned away. I can just see him drained and frustrated yelling out: "C'mon! You have got to be kidding!"

But even when we just don't get it, there is a reason — a reason that is very important for followers of Christ to embrace — and it's that God's ways are not our ways (Isaiah 55:8). If we believe God is formulaic, that we can predict His plan, that we can somehow manipulate a certain outcome, that we can even understand the things that do happen, we will be frustrated, and our faith will be impeded.

Instead, the clear message of the Bible is that God is Sovereign and God is good. Lon Solomon, pastor of McLean Bible Church, paints the picture this way. He says that God is looking at the whole parade that makes up our lives, not just some tiny portion. The things that happen in our snippet of the parade may not seem to make a lick of sense. But if we were able to see our whole parade, like God does, we could see that it is all for our good and His glory. Two thousand years later, we can see that it was a good plan for Jesus to be born in a stable. Mary and Joseph got to be in a place where the shepherds could come and see the newborn King, and it beautifully illustrates the humility of Christ.

But maybe you are facing something today, where you think, okay God, why didn't you just cause this to happen or that to not? But we are blessed when we take God at His Word. He says that He has a plan (Jeremiah 29:11), and He promises that for those who love Him, that all things work together for good (Romans 8:28).

Yes, even if you are facing a situation today that feels like you are being turned away and abandoned in an hour of need, God promises to use it for your good and His Glory.

Recommended Scripture

Ephesians 3: 14-21

Questions for Reflection

Where in your life do you have trouble believing that God has a good plan? How can you take Him at His Word? Can you *choose* to believe that His love for you is deeper than you can possibly even grasp?

Closing Prayer

*Heavenly Father, help me to be submitted to Your will for my life today, and help me to trust You in **all** things. In Jesus' Name, Amen.*

DECEMBER 4
"COME TO ME"

Even though I've experienced loss — my father passed away in 1999 and my brother in 2002 — the suddenness of their deaths meant that I never watched them suffer physically. I'm sure the emotional toll of watching someone you love suffer is immense. Be it slow and painful, or sudden and catastrophic, it seems like every year I know someone facing tremendous heartache at Christmas.

But whether you are someone who is facing something truly tragic and life-altering, or someone whose current concerns seem less earth-shattering, we need to remember that God cares about whatever we care about. Jesus said, "Come to me, *all* who are weary and burdened, and I will give you rest" (Matthew 11: 28). He didn't say, He'd give rest for heavy burdens only, or rest for people who get their lives in some semblance of order first. He didn't say He'd grant rest to some people or some of the time. No, Jesus is ever-willing to give us rest. But there is one requirement:

we need to *come* to Him.

The stiff-necked won't. No one comes with a puffed-up posture. Only the humble come. Only those who know they cannot do it on their own.

I know a swim coach who has a pretty magical connection with kids. I'm sure you know someone like this man, someone whose magnetism for youth is almost inexplicable, someone who engenders crazed adoration. This man doesn't exude warmth and love to adults -- I'm not the only grown-up who finds him somewhat hard to engage. But every teenager and child he meets seems to fall in line with undying devotion.

And honestly, I get it. For one thing, he's real. He expects things of his swimmers and tells them how they can achieve their goals. He believes in them. He told me one time about how he encouraged his young swimmers before an important meet. He gave them 3 x 5 cards and told them to write down what about the swim meet had them worried. Some were worried they would false start. Some were worried they would forget to do this or that, others had other kinds of fears. The coach put the worries in a jar. He told his swimmers to let go of their fears because he was holding onto all the fears for them. Even though my own swimmer sons were not part of this event, this little story touched my heart, because it was such a loving gesture!

It also gives us a tiny glimpse of what it's like to cast all our cares and burdens on Jesus. He loves us unconditionally each and every day, and He cares about whatever we care about. He wants to hold our fears, worries and concerns and give us rest. He wants us to *be* and to *feel* totally unburdened. May we know His rest in a new and deeper way this season.

Recommended Scripture:

Matthew 11: 28-30

Questions for Reflection

What are you burdened about today? What typically makes you worry? What keeps you from bringing your concerns to Jesus? When you do cast your fears at His feet how do you feel?

Closing Prayer

Heavenly Father, may your sustaining grace be real to those whose hearts are broken today by loss. May I know your restorative rest in my own life. May I not miss the opportunity to have You help me carry my burdens, whether they are heavy or light. May I be humble enough each day to Come to You! In Jesus' Name, Amen.

DECEMBER 5
WONDER. LOVE. AND PRAISE.

So much emotion can be wrapped up in a melody — a few notes can unlock a flood of memories, a jingle can take us back to a certain place and time we had nearly forgotten. Christmas music, as part of a steady annual tradition, can be both more and less profound than ordinary music. It's more profound because it celebrates the birth of Our Savior, and because artists over the centuries have devoted some of their best efforts to it. But sometimes it's less profound because it is so familiar. We know the words, but do we meditate on them?

Very small children can hum the melody to Beethoven's Ode to Joy, but how deeply do the words resonate with us, familiar as they are? Here are the words, by Linda Lee Johnson:

Joyful, joyful, we adore You, God of glory, Lord of light. Angels lifting praise before You Sing thro'out this holy night. In a manger lies a Baby — Child of Mary, Son of God. Voices joined in joyful chorus Praise You for Your gift of love.

All Your works declare Your glory; All creation joins to sing, Praise resounds as earth rejoices In the birth of Christ, the King. Shepherds kneel before the Infant. Trumpets sound and anthems raise. As with joy our hearts are lifted. Joined in wonder, love and praise.

Christmas lights are beautiful — I can never get enough of them — but may they prompt me to reflect on The Lord of Light, Who figuratively and literally makes darkness flee. When I see representations of the cherub-faced baby, may I stop to contemplate the miracle — C.S. Lewis called it the Grand Miracle [3]— that this baby was somehow the child of Mary, but also the Son of God. May this be a season of joy, and may my heart be lifted, joined with all Christ-followers in wonder, love and praise.

Recommended Scripture

Luke 2

Questions for Reflection

Where in your life are you reluctant to shine the Light of Christ? In what circumstances are you most likely to experience wonder? Love? Praise? Do you see how the above questions are related? Can we ever experience wonder, love or praise in the dark where Christ is not?

Closing Prayer

Heavenly Father, help me to embrace the Light of Christ in all areas of my life. May I be filled to overflowing with wonder, love and praise. In Jesus' Name, Amen.

---

[3] C.S. Lewis, *God in the Dock*, (London: Eerdmans, 1970).

DECEMBER 6
A RESOUNDING GONG

This time of year we hear so much about stress, and for some it is completely self-inflicted. There is so much hurry, hurry. One Thursday in December 2013, I experienced the following snippet of parenting.

"C'mon," I yelled to my then ten-year-old. "What are you doing? Help me out. Carry all that to the car. You'll need to make two trips!" And as he tried to carry it all in one trip, I issued another snippy and exasperated, "Two trips, Nate!"

What made this example especially noteworthy wasn't that I was snippy and impatient –unfortunately, that is not terribly uncommon. But we happened to be hurrying off to a charity event, a charity event that some friends and I had organized. But I sure wasn't being too charitable to my own son. We had looked forward to this because it was a "Throwback Thursday" Basketball Game to raise funds for a local food pantry, and my two oldest sons were both playing in it. By God's undeserved grace, we got the car packed up with all the throwback shorts and socks in time for me to take a deep breath, regain my composure and thoroughly enjoy the event.

But in Corinthians, Paul writes that your great feats do not matter in the least if you do not have love. If you do not have love, you are like a "resounding gong or clanging cymbal" (1 Corinthians 13:1 NIV). I remember *The Gong Show* from the 70's and I know I do not want to be like a resounding gong, nor do I want to be a clanging anything, but especially not a cymbal. The most important thing I can do is not to get through my list or ensure I'm following through on all the commitments I've made, but to be loving in the moment. Because if I'm not, I'm a resounding gong.

May I ponder these verses and live by them:

Love is patient and kind; love does not envy or boast; it is not arrogant or rude. It does not insist on its own way; it is not irritable or resentful; it does not rejoice at wrongdoing, but rejoices with the truth. Love bears all things, believes all things, hopes all things, endures all things. 1 Corinthians 13: 4-7

Recommended Scripture
1 Corinthians 13

Questions for Reflection
When you entertain or prepare for an event is there a frenzied, gong-like vibe? What causes you to be impatient? In what ways can you avoid creating situations where you are most inclined to clang like a cymbal?

Closing Prayer
Heavenly Father, forgive me for being impatient, for being a clanging cymbal, for keeping records of wrongs, for being self-seeking. Help me to be loving in each moment. Lord, I know I can only do that as a reflection of You, so help me to live by and through the Holy Spirit each and every day. In Jesus' Name, Amen.

DECEMBER 7
TRUMPETS

My husband and I got married at Christmastime – December 29, 1995. On either side of the altar stood artificial Christmas trees that we purchased to add to the meager decorations inside the little chapel. My mom and I decorated them with an abundance of white lights, wine-colored poinsettias, miniature brass angels and musical instruments as ornaments. We each kept a tree and the decorations. For years I used that tree and decorated it just like it was at my wedding, but eventually the years caught up with the tree and I bid it farewell. I still have the decorations though – the poinsettias and shiny angels, violins and trumpets are brought out every year.

Music is such a vital part of the season. You couldn't avoid Christmas music if you wanted to – you can hardly turn on the radio or walk into a store without the sounds of the season greeting you. So I love hanging my little instruments on the tree or around the house. Although I will say that even though I find the violin beautiful, it is always a little melancholy. I mean, cartoon characters break it out for pity parties for a reason. But what would be the opposite instrument? What sound is just plain *happy*? Steel drums, maybe? It's almost hard not to imagine a hammock under a palm tree when you hear steel drums. But one of the happiest sounds, for me, is the trumpet. I love the sound of the trumpet – clear and strong and happy, and I love my little trumpet ornaments.

For many years, I've had the privilege of hearing a brass quintet from The President's Own Marine Band perform a miniature Christmas concert at my sons' school. I can't even tell you how much I enjoy this tradition. Two trumpets, a trombone, a French horn, and a tuba – what a joyful noise! They typically play Tchaikovsky and O Holy Night and Sleigh Ride, among others. Good live music is balm for the soul. We should soak in the beautiful music of the season as much as we possibly can.

Of course, the Bible reveals a special role for the trumpet, which may have something to do with my thirst for its sound. In Revelation, it says that one day the trumpet will sound, and when it does, Jesus will reign for ever and ever (11: 15). No more sadness, no more tears, just Jesus ruling. Forever and ever. Can you stop today and try to imagine what it will be like to hear that trumpet? We can picture the fairy tale's trumpeter announcing the arrival of the dashing prince, but can we imagine the trumpet signally the real and promised arrival of The Kingdom of Jesus?

May we prepare our hearts to celebrate His birth with an eye toward the promise that He will reign forever and ever.

Recommended Scripture

Psalm 40

Questions for Reflection

What are a few or your favorite Christmas songs? Why are they special to you?

Closing Prayer

Heavenly Father, thank you for music — for how it speaks to us so deeply, how it can connect our hearts, speak truth, and buoy our spirits. Thank you that you have gifted so many people with a special talent for playing music, and thank you for opportunities to hear great music, especially at Christmastime. In Jesus' Name, Amen.

DECEMBER 8
THE UNUSED GIFT

Have you ever *given* a gift you are quite certain has never been used? Have you ever *received* a gift that you've never put to use? I think honesty probably requires a "yes" on both counts, right? We could analyze why this happens (compulsory gift-giving? underutilization of the gift card?), but no matter the why, the result is the same: an unused gift is sad. In fact, the more sacrificial or extravagant the gift, the sadder its lack of use becomes. How horribly tragic then is the unwrapped or even blatantly rejected gift of salvation, meaning, and purpose offered through Jesus Christ. Who in their right mind would turn down love and forgiveness? Or an explanation for where we came from and why we are here? Who would turn down an offer to spend eternity with an all-loving Creator? Who would turn down the greatest gift ever given (John 3:16)?

As it turns out, a lot of people. Pride gets in the way. People don't want to humble themselves to admit they've been wrong. They don't want to admit they fall short (Romans 3:23). They don't want to live life according to anyone's rules but their own (Romans 1:18-32). But as followers of Christ, we should never be puffed up into thinking we don't make this same mistake. Because we do, in at least a couple different ways.

First, we've been given the gift of the Holy Spirit, and yet we don't rely on Him as we should. How often do we actively seek to live in accordance with His faithful prodding and direction (Galatians 5: 13-26)? I know that I would be a more godly woman if I was faithful to listen more closely to the Holy Spirit, to seek His counsel more actively throughout my day. So why don't I do it? Well, I'm just like the unbeliever — somewhere deep inside, my own stubborn will is saying, "I got this."

Of course the truth is I'm never going to be more loving, joyful, peace-filled, patient, kind, good, faithful, gentle, or self-controlled without the power of the Holy Spirit living in me. So during this season of gift-opening, may I daily open the gift that is the ever-present counsel of the Holy Spirit.

Recommended Scripture
Galatians 5

Questions for Reflection
Can you think of an example of a gift you gave that went unused? Is there any bitterness over this that you need to release to God? Are you doing a good job of tapping into the power of the Holy Spirit? How can you be more faithful in listening to His still small voice in day-to-day life?

Closing Prayer
Heavenly Father, may I live by the Spirit, open all the gifts you have for me, and not miss blessings because of my own persistent pride. Thank you for loving me despite my failures. In Jesus' name, Amen.

DECEMBER 9
MORE UNUSED GIFTS

Yesterday's reading was about rejecting God's greatest gifts for us, but there is a different, less gravely offensive way that we can fail to use the gifts we've been given. No one wants to see unwrapped gifts scattered haphazardly around the tree — trinkets and ties accepted but quickly forgotten. It feels wasteful. But if a beautifully personalized gift was never used, just carelessly tossed out with the wrapping paper, that would be even worse, wouldn't it?

Yet the Bible says we've been given unique gifts. Romans 12:6-8 says, "We have different gifts, according to the grace given to each of us. If your gift is prophesying, then prophesy in accordance with your faith; if it is serving, then serve; if it is teaching, then teach; if it is to encourage, then give encouragement; if it is giving, then give generously; if it is to lead, do it diligently; if it is to show mercy, do it cheerfully." In sum, whatever your gift is, use it!

Are you an encourager? Do you like to serve others? Are you a teacher? A leader? Then encourage, serve, teach and lead. Strive to be great at these things. Invest time and energy in growing your gifts – pray for wisdom and for opportunities to use them. In my own life, I believe writing is both a passion and a gift. I devote lots of time to developing this gift. I write frequently. I study writing by reading books on writing. I ask others for feedback. I try to use this gift for God's glory.

This season, if you witness someone open a beautifully wrapped present that is just perfect for that person, think how sad it would be for the giver if the recipient never used this gift, and instead just kicked it to the back of the closet, never to be seen again.

Might this be how God feels about the gifts He has given you? May we know our gifts, and use them all for His glory.

Recommended Scripture

Romans 12:3-8

Questions for Reflection

Do you know what your gifts are? Do you use them? How can you encourage your family members and close friends to utilize their gifts?

Closing Prayer

Heavenly Father, thank you for the gifts you've given me. May I be grateful to have them and eager to use them for Your glory. May I be wise and discerning in helping those around me to know their gifts, and may I faithfully encourage each of them to use these gifts. In Jesus' name, Amen.

DECEMBER 10
AN ADVENT OF FAITH

Oswald Chambers, in his wonderful little devotional, *My Utmost for His Highest*, refers to the birth of Jesus like this: "His life is the Highest and the Holiest entering in at the Lowliest door. Our Lord's birth was an advent."[4] Reading this the first time made me feel like I might not even know the meaning of the word "advent."

For me, the word denotes anticipation and waiting for the arrival of Christ, of His birth. But the dictionary definition is a little broader. It says that advent is "a coming into place, view, or being." Chambers must have meant that Jesus' birth was a coming into place (the earth) and a coming into view. But he *definitely* didn't mean a coming into being. Because Jesus

---

[4] Oswald Chambers, *My Utmost for His Highest* (Grand Rapids: Discovery House, 1935), December 25th.

has always been and will always be (Hebrews 13:8). During this season, I have a heavy-heartedness for my friends who do not know the comfort and peace this Truth provides. I wonder what Christmas is about for them — does it feel like an empty dressing up of false hope, a forced wonder at twinkling lights that don't really represent anything?

As I look outside and cloudless blue skies seem even brighter against winter's white snow, I am awed by God's majesty. It leads me to pray that my friends who do not know Jesus as Lord and Savior will contemplate Him in a new way this season. May they have their own advent this year, the advent of saving faith.

You might try specifically praying John 1: 1- 5 for unbelieving friends. Pray these words will ring true in their hearts:

In the beginning was the Word, and the Word was with God, and the Word was God. He was with God in the beginning. Through him all things were made; without him nothing was made that has been made. In him was life, and that life was the light of all mankind. The light shines in the darkness, and the darkness has not overcome it.

And that perhaps their journey would be something like Sheldon Vanauken, the author of A *Severe Mercy*. Here is an excerpt of his chapter, "Encounter with Light," which describes the advent of his own faith.

I choose to believe in the Father, Son, and Holy Ghost — in Christ, my lord and my God. Christianity has the ring, the feel, of unique truth. Of essential truth. By it, life is made full instead of empty, meaningful instead of meaningless... A choice was necessary: and there is no certainty. One can only choose a side. So I — I now choose my side: I choose beauty; I choose what I love. But choosing to believe is believing. It's all I can do: choose.[5]

Recommended Scripture

Mark 9:14-29

Questions for Reflection

What causes you to have doubts about your faith? Have you ever cried out to God, asking Him to help you in your unbelief? How do you pray for your friends who do not have Jesus in their lives?

Closing Prayer

Heavenly Father, move in the hearts of my friends who do not know You. May I be a good ambassador. Forgive me for my failings in this responsibility, and help me to be better each day. Help my friends realize that they have a choice, and that as Vanauken says choosing to believe is believing. May they choose you, and may they know it's not about never having any doubts. Instead, may we all say together, Lord, I believe, help me overcome my unbelief! In Jesus' Name, Amen.

---

[5] Sheldon Vanauken, *A Severe Mercy: A Story of Faith, Tragedy and Triumph* (Harper Collins: New York, 1977), 99.

DECEMBER 11
GRACE AND TRUTH

My friend Holly is about the most joyful, life-giving, affirming person on earth. When I see her, or even just hear her voice, my day is invariably brightened. And let me tell you it's not because she isn't willing to cause a stir or call a spade a spade. She is. So it's fitting that Holly is also the person who I've heard most succinctly explain the balance between two forces that sometimes *feel* like opposite poles of an imaginary continuum.

Holly says that we need to view truth and grace (truth and love/justice and mercy) as the two wings of an airplane. Your plane isn't going anywhere with one wing — whether it's easier for you to embrace the truth wing, or the grace wing. Planes just don't fly with one wing. And if you think seriously for a minute about your closest friends you can probably pick out a few that favor one wing over the other — where one wing tends to be their go-to, their default. But most of us embrace whatever wing is convenient for our circumstance. If we are the wrongdoer, well then, grace it is! But if we've been wronged, oh how we pine for justice. But the perfection of these ideals truth/justice on one side and grace/mercy/love on the other are not truly weights on a scale, or opposing forces in any way — they are two aspects of the Person of Jesus Christ (John 1: 14). The Cross represents both the mercy of God and His wrath — justice and love are perfected at Calvary.

The song *Joy to the World* is sung at Christmastime, because it is a song which celebrates the birth of Christ, but it is also a song that anticipates when Jesus will rule the earth.

> *He rules the earth with truth and grace,*
> *and makes the nations prove*
> *the glories of his righteousness*
> *and wonders of his love*
> *and wonders of his love*
> *and wonders of his love*

Truth and Grace. Glories of His Righteousness and Wonders of His Love. May today we recognize that Jesus embodies and perfects both truth and grace.

Recommended Scripture

John 1

Questions for Reflection

Where do you need grace right now? Where do you long for justice?

Closing Prayer

Heavenly Father, may I be a reflection of You. May I be willing to speak the truth in love. May I be righteous and merciful. May I not let this world convince me that these are two endpoints on a continuum — instead may I live in the assurance that these are two aspects of You. May I know and live the glories of Your righteousness, and the wonders of Your love. In Jesus' Name, Amen.

DECEMBER 12
A REFINING FIRE

C.S. Lewis wrote, "it seems to me that one can hardly say anything either bad enough or good enough about life."[6] Do you ever feel like that? Do ever feel like there aren't really words to adequately describe the simple joys in life? And yet at the same time, it's hard to express how painful life can be? Despite the window dressing, the posts on social media, the seemingly endlessly stream of perfect-looking families sending out charming cards at Christmas, the heartaches of life are never put on hold. Even if you find yourself sailing on relatively peaceful waters, surely you have family and friends who are battling dark days.

Faith may be easy in a sunny meadow, but it can't compare to the battle-scarred faith of a saint who has endured. We need to regularly lift up

---

[6] C.S. Lewis, *Letter of C.S. Lewis* (February 8, 1956).

the hurting, praying that their faith, as well as our own faith, will be like refined silver — more beautiful and reflective of Christ *because* of the fire (Malachi 3).

I don't understand how secular people endure the nagging questions, the inexplicable pain. How can the sorrow of cancer, of death, of evil be faced through the prism that this is *all* there is?

Which brings me back to Jesus in the stable. His humble birth is the promise that this *isn't* all there is. As the angels announced to the shepherds, " Today in the town of David a Savior has been born to you; he is the Messiah, the Lord" (Luke 2:11). We celebrate Christmas because it marks the birth of our Savior.

But what does Christ our Savior save us from? Meaninglessness, condemnation, and separation from God for starters. But Jesus is never going to force Himself on you. We need to accept Him.

In what areas are you refusing His help? There must be some part of your life where all is not well, where you just don't have the answers. May we start with those things — handing over to God our burdens, and as we grow in faith we can give him our doubts, our deepest questions, and at some point in time, our everything. May Jesus be Lord over all of it, the too wonderful for words and the too painful to fully comprehend. And then may we recommit ourselves to Him again and again and again, saying: Jesus, You are Lord.

The Bible says that God's mercies are new every morning (Lamentations 3:22-23). I am in awe of and grateful for this truth. I believe we are destined to either live in denial of the brokenness around us, or we are going to sometimes feel almost crushed by its reality. Sometimes even in a single day there are dramatic highs and lows — the joys of life in stark contrast to its brutal pain. The discipline is to remind yourself of the truth every single day, to turn to Him every single day.

May we embrace His mercies and give ourselves to Him today and every day.

Recommended Scripture

Lamentations 3:22-24

Questions for Reflection

What do you need to be saved from this Christmas? How can you claim God's mercies in this area?

Closing Prayer

Heavenly Father, thank you that your mercies never end. Help me to daily recommit my life to You and to live by the Holy Spirit every minute of every day. Thank you for loving me. In Jesus' Name, Amen.

DECEMBER 13
THE GLORY OF CHRISTMAS

"Glory" is a word we hear a lot this time of year, from singing "Glory to the newborn King" to using all forms — glories, glorious and glorify. The much-anticipated annual program at a church I sometimes attend in Michigan is called "The Glory of Christmas." Come December, the word is practically everywhere.

But what does "glory" actually mean? Perhaps it's predictable that the dictionary has no shortage of definitions. My two favorites are perhaps the simplest: (1) adoring praise /worshipful thanksgiving; and (2) resplendent beauty/magnificence. If you combine these, that's how I'd like my house to be during Advent, full of adoring praise, worshipful thanksgiving, and resplendent beauty. And of course, my family and I fall short – way short – every year. But we do have glimpses of adoring praise and worshipful thanksgiving – our tree is usually gorgeous, I love buying giant poinsettias from Costco, we talk about what we are thankful for, and my husband insists that we listen to classical Christmas music for weeks.

But if you believe the Bible, which teaches that each person is made in the image of God (Genesis 1:27), then it is important for us to treat one another with a certain degree of glory too.

I love what C.S. Lewis says in *The Weight of Glory*:

> *It may be possible for each to think too much of his own potential glory hereafter; it is hardly possible for him to think too often or too deeply about that of his neighbour. The load, or weight, or burden of my neighbour's glory should be laid on my back, a load so heavy that only humility can carry it, and the backs of the proud will be broken.*[7]

What a paradigm shift! We can't think too much about the glory of our neighbors? Then I've got some serious work to do.

Lewis also writes that we can hardly fathom the delight of our Creator over His creation.

> *To please God…to be the real ingredient in the divine happiness…to be loved by God, not merely pitied, but delighted in as an artist delights in his work or a father in a son — it seems impossible, a weight or burden of glory which our thoughts can hardly sustain. But so it is.*[8]

The weight of glory, yes, we can hardly fathom it, but so it is. May we respond with adoring thanks and worshipful praise!

Recommended Scripture

Genesis 1:26-28

---

[7] C.S. Lewis, *The Weight of Glory*, (Harper Collins: New York, 1949), 45.
[8] Ibid, 39.

Questions for Reflection

Who in your life is hard to love? Have you thought lately that this person was made in the image of God? Have you considered too that your Creator delights over you as an artist over his very best work?

Closing Prayer

Heavenly Father, may I treasure the truth that you love me, may I show Your love to others, and may Your Name be glorified in my house not just during Christmas, but every day of the year. In Jesus' Name, Amen.

DECEMBER 14
A COMMON PRAYER

I do not often consult my copy of the *Book of Common Prayer*, but whenever I hear prayers read from it, I am invariably struck by both the depth and the beauty of the language. And I find it comforting to know that followers of Jesus here in America have used this little book as a guide to prayer for centuries.

I was flipping through it on December 14, 2013 -- the somber first anniversary of the Sandy Hook massacre. I came across the following prayer for social justice, which continues to strike just the right tone.

Almighty God, who hast created us in thine own image; Grant us grace fearlessly to contend against evil and to make no peace with oppression; and, that we may reverently use our freedom, help us to employ it in the maintenance of justice in our communities and among the nations, to the glory of thy holy Name; through Jesus Christ our Lord, who liveth and reigneth with thee and the Holy Spirit, one God.

May we pray today for families around the world that are grieving the loss of their child. I cannot fathom the pain that is endured by parents when the life of their child is intentionally taken. It's too horrific for words. And yet we know that celebrating the birth of Jesus does not mean that all was set right in the world — few events better illustrate the fallen state in which we continue to live better than the atrocity committed on 12/14/12. But the hope Jesus provides is an *offer* given to all, given to the world. John 3:16 says, "For God so loved the world, that he gave his only Son, that whoever believes in him should not perish but have eternal life."

Offers by definition require a response. Each person who is able says "yes," or they say "no." Those who are of sound mind and maturity and yet pretend not to answer, are really rejecting Christ's offer. May we pray that we can be salt and light that leads people closer to "yes." May we be faithful ambassadors for Christ. May we pray for those in our lives who are still searching.

May today we be willing to renew our grateful "Yes!" May we remember that "God gave us a spirit not of fear but of power and love and self-control" (2 Timothy 1:7). May we be bold in contending with evil, faithful to use our freedom to secure and maintain justice, and to do it through Jesus Christ and for Jesus Christ.

Recommended Scripture

2 Timothy 1:6-14

Questions for Reflection

Who in your life has lost a child? How can you love that person today? How can you contend with evil in your every day life?

Closing Prayer

Heavenly Father, comfort the hurting today, give them a special measure of your peace, and help me to be salt and light in the world for You. In Jesus' name, Amen.

DECEMBER 15
AN ENTITLEMENT MENTALITY

We greet each and every day with certain expectations, but Christmas morning is often a day with inflated expectations. Of course, there is no more consistent formula for disappointment than setting unrealistic expectations, and everyone's expectations are fueled by absurd marketing schemes this time of year. From the giant-bowed luxury car to the larger-than-life diamonds – everyone on television seems to be receiving extravagant gifts in surroundings that are nothing short of magical. It's not like they show the unveiling of the car in pouring rain, with a drippy bow – but that would be bound to happen some of the time if luxury cars were routinely given as Christmas gifts.

Mid-December is a perfect time to take a step back and ask ourselves some questions. What are my expectations? What kind of pressure am I putting on those around me? Are there grandiose expectations of me that I can never meet? Where does my sense of entitlement come from? Deep down, what do I believe that I deserve?

Thomas á Kempis wrote on this more than five centuries ago. Instead of feeling entitled, he was hyperaware of his own sinfulness, of his unworthiness.

He wrote directly to the Lord:

> *Though I might weep the water of tears like to the sea, I would not be worthy to have Your solace. I am worthy to have nothing but sorrow and pain, for I have so grievously and so often offended You and in so many things trespassed against You....I do not know that I have done anything as well as I should, though I do know that I have always been prone and ready to sin and slow to amend...Humble contrition of heart is to You, O Lord, a most acceptable sacrifice, which savors more sweetly in Your sight than burning incense.*[9]

Thomas á Kempis believed he deserved nothing, nothing but sorrow and pain. Think about that! I doubt Christmas morning was a disappointment at the á Kempis household. But what can we learn from that kind of humility? Well, a lot. The more we are aware of the darkness in our own hearts, the more grateful we become. We are sometimes prone to think, "Well, I'm not as bad as *that* person." But other people are not the standard. Christ is the standard. Perfection is the standard. And the more we realize how grievous our own sins are, the more we can appreciate the price that Jesus paid to restore us.

Jesus summarized it perfectly when he talked about the "sinful woman." He said: "Therefore I tell you, her sins, which are many, are forgiven—for she loved much. But he who is forgiven little, loves little" (Luke 7:47).

---

[9] Thomas á Kempis, *The Imitation of Christ* (Edited by Harold C. Gardiner), (New York: Doubleday, 1955), 183-184.

May we be aware this season of our own sins. Not so that we can beat ourselves up, but so that we might know the degree to which we've been forgiven. In short, may we love much and expect little.

Recommended Scripture

Luke 7:41-50

Questions for Reflection

Do you ever find yourself thinking that you are a "good" person or measuring your sins or good deeds against someone else's? How can you point yourself back to Jesus instead? When in your life have you felt like you loved God the most? Do you think it had anything to do with being forgiven?

Closing Prayer

Heavenly Father, help me to know the depths of my own sin, so that You can shine Your redeeming light in every dark corner. Thank you, Lord, for loving me and forgiving me, even though I sometimes act entitled. Help me to be grateful every day and to live for You. In Jesus' name, Amen.

DECEMBER 16
HARAKA HARAKA HAINA BARAKA

I am amazing at one thing. I know it might sound boastful but I am. What is it? Doing really embarrassing things.

One morning in December of 2013, I went to Target. I was on a mission and knocking things off my list left and right. But all of a sudden, in the snack food aisle, I realized that I had inexplicably worn khaki pants, a solid red shirt, topped with a solid red sweater. I am not kidding! I went to Target in uniform. And my uniform did not escape notice. In fact, it was the general manger who called me out on it.

In fact, I was sort of a spectacle because I had a *very* full cart that had a 20″ boy's bike teetering on top. Plus I'm six-feet-tall, plus the uniform. Anyway, as I was standing in the checkout line, the manager, Dave, said, "Do you have a RED card?"

"I think I used to," I said.

Then he explained to me why I should have one again, and I agreed.

"Plus," Dave said, "You have the red and khaki. I like it."

I laughed — what else could I do?

Then Dave said to the cashier, "Can you go ahead and process the RED card? Or do you have to wait till you ring everything up?"

"Oh, I'm not in any hurry," I said.

Dave looked at me stunned. "You're not?" he said. "I always assume everyone is in a hurry this time of year – pretty refreshing to encounter someone who isn't."

Now, I have to admit that "I'm not in a hurry" is not a refrain I am often caught using, but I *really* wasn't in a hurry. My boys were at school after a string of snow days, and I felt like it was a me-time indulgence to linger in Target for a little while.

Dave ended up walking me out to my car and loading the bike for me. It turned out that he and I have a tremendous Target history together. He lived in Canton, Michigan (the area where I grew up) and he managed the Reston, Virginia store (the store I walked to with great frequency when I had just one son). I mean this guy and I have crossed paths for decades. And he raised three sons. How funny that a little phrase like "I'm not in a hurry" caused all these connections to be made.

Or is it funny? Is it instead totally predictable? The Swahili saying, "haraka haraka haina baraka" means hurry hurry has no blessings.

May we not hurry through the blessings God has for us this season. May we instead number our days aright and gain a heart of wisdom (Psalm 90:12).

Recommended Scripture

Psalm 90

Questions for Reflection

Can you think of time that lingering in the moment brought unusual blessing? How can you hurry less and be present in the moment more?

Closing Prayer

Heavenly Father, thank you for the humility embarrassing situations amply supply. Help me not to hurry past the blessings you have for me. Help me to slow down and daily live an unhurried life that reflects You. In Jesus' Name, Amen.

DECEMBER 17
A DIFFERENT KIND OF LIST

Some people know exactly what types of gifts they want for Christmas. My son, Sam, shared a very detailed list with Santa in 2013: Mario Kart 7, a remote-controlled Jeep, and a Nerf gun. In fact, coming up with specifics for *wants* is not generally very challenging for any of us.

But how about things we already have? How detailed are we about gratitude? Because being detailed about gratitude is actually more important than being detailed about wants. Think about it: if we just say, yes, I'm thankful for my life, for all my blessings, we are painting with broad, quick strokes, and it doesn't engender the deepest gratitude. It's speedy and painless, and better than nothing, but Charles Edward Jefferson said, "Gratitude is born in hearts that take time to count up past mercies." I love this quote. I want to grow and nourish a grateful heart by counting up past mercies with specificity.

During this busy season when shopping lists, Christmas card lists, and wish lists pervade, may we take the time to write out a different kind of list, a list that counts up past mercies. May we think seriously and specifically about how we are thankful for the blessings we already have.

Obviously, there has been no shortage of songwriters and authors who repeat this simple but transformative message: count your blessings. But when is the last time you made a literal list? Do you have one somewhere? You can scribble down a few specifics anywhere, anytime, or you can keep them in a more permanent place too. I do it all different ways. I have a special journal for recording events in my life where I see God's Hand most vividly — I do not want to lose or forget those. Ever. But any counting up of mercies will bless you and change your outlook for the better. Why not take a minute right now to scribble down five things from today?

These are the five I wrote down in December 2013:

1. The way Sam is utterly delighted with himself by his progress as a reader.
2. The way my husband walked around the mall with us tonight, unaided. After knee surgery and a long recovery, a tireless walk around the mall is a true milestone.
3. The sound of Nate's laugh, and how much I heard it today sledding.
4. How gorgeous snow is, and how it brings the DC area to a screeching halt.
5. That even though it's cold outside, we have a warm house to call our own.

May the busyness of our December days not rob us of the habit of gratitude. Instead, may we be thankful in all circumstances, just like the Bible says (1 Thessalonians 5:18). May the anticipation of Christmas increase our gratitude, not our wish lists.

Recommended Scripture

1 Thessalonians 5:12-28

Questions for Reflection

Have you ever made a written list of things for which you are grateful? How did it change your outlook? Why don't you do this more often?

Closing Prayer

Heavenly Father, help me to be grateful. Help me to give thanks in all things and to be transformed by the renewing of my mind. May I listen to the still small voice of the Holy Spirit Who prompts me to give thanks. In Jesus' Name, Amen.

DECEMBER 18
SIGNING OVER THE TITLE

My friend Tom Tarrants wrote a wonderful article on living a surrendered life that I highly recommend reading in full.[10] There is no better time to think about committing, or recommitting, your life to Christ than at Christmastime. The primary text for the article is Romans 12:1-2, which has been tremendously life-altering for me. The first verse talks about offering our bodies as living sacrifices, holy and pleasing to God, as a spiritual act of worship.

Tom writes, "Unfortunately in the past century many well-meaning believers have seen this text as something akin to the U.S. Army appealing to its regular troops for volunteers for the special forces…giv[ing] the impression that Paul is calling believers to an *optional* higher level of

---

[10] Thomas A. Tarrants III, *What God Wants from You* (Knowing & Doing, Winter 2013).

commitment" (emphasis mine). Instead Tom argues that a sold-out, spirit-led level of commitment *should* be the norm. And I agree. Was Jesus not more than vivid about how He feels about people who are lukewarm? He says He will *spit* them out (Revelation 3:16)!

Yet somehow, we are so reluctant to give God all of ourselves that we have endless excuses to hold this part back or that part back. Matthew Henry wrote in his commentary on this verse, that we need to transfer to God all right, title and interest.[11] What a thought-provoking concept!

Have you ever signed over a title? We traded in my husband's car in November of 2013. We brought the existing title with us along to the dealership. There is a sense of gravity in that. We had owned that trusty old car for a long time, brought babies home in it. It had been good to us. Even though we were getting a brand new car with all the latest gadgets and gizmos, we were reluctant to let go of the old one. Of course, in the end, we signed it over without trying to argue that maybe we could keep the sunroof or hold onto the soft, worn leather. We just signed it over. Period.

Have you done that with your life? Have you given it over completely to God? We all need to do this at a moment in time. I've written elsewhere about my "signing over" which took place on 10/22/2006. We will always need to keep relinquishing our lives every day, but you should know the day you said to God for the first time and without reservation, "here it is, my whole life, it belongs to you."

We celebrate the birth of Jesus in just seven days. How wonderful

---

[11] Matthew Henry, *Commentary on the Whole Bible* (Peabody: Henderickson Publishers, 1991), 1781.

would it be this year to rejoice in knowing you've signed over your life to the Person who knows you best and loves you most?

Recommended Scripture

Romans 12:1-2

Questions for Reflection

Have you committed your life to Christ by signing over all right, title and interest? How can you daily recommit your life to Christ?

Closing Prayer

Heavenly Father, thank you for loving me. Help me to live a surrendered life, to make surrender a daily commitment and to rejoice in knowing that you have a good plan for my life. In Jesus' Name, Amen.

DECEMBER 19
A LIST YOU WANT TO BE ON

Every day, whether we acknowledge it or not, we have a standing invitation from Jesus to come to Him, to lay our burdens on His strong and compassionate shoulders. Over the last two thousand years, a list has been building of people who've come to Jesus with their burdens, their worries, their messed up situations and found rest, peace and compassion. The shepherds from that very first Christmas top the list, but other early mentions include wise men from the East, John – Jesus' cousin – who heralded repentance, and a certain twelve disciples, including the rugged individualist Peter and his brother Andrew, who were fishermen by trade. Then there were crowds who came in daylight, and timid followers like Nicodemus who came by cover of night. Some came to Jesus with shame, some with physical pain, some with unspeakable loss. Thousands humbly came to Jesus and found him to be loving, compassionate and powerful.

Yet some in Scripture met Jesus and walked away troubled and discouraged. The rich young ruler left "very sad" – no, he didn't want to sell all he had (Luke 18). The Pharisees were none too pleased by their encounters with Jesus either — after all, He criticized their legalism and unloving ways.

Many today reject Jesus too. They say that Jesus never claimed to be God (they haven't read very much Scripture if they make this claim), and they find Him too exclusivist. Jesus boldly claimed to be "the way, and the truth, and the life" and that "no one comes to the Father except through" Him (John 14:6).

Jesus offers: "Come to Me." But many do not want to humble themselves or they do not want to change (like the rich young ruler who had no interest in giving up his wealth, many reject Jesus because of His requirements). I know people who put up an incredible fight. They just don't want Jesus to be the answer. Maybe it's cultural. Maybe they don't want to let go of their bitterness. Maybe they just abhor the idea of aligning themselves with the Christians they know (that's an entirely different problem — Christians will always be imperfect, but our imperfections cannot be imputed to Christ). Most of the bricks are rooted in pride,[12] but no matter the source, people keep reinforcing that wall of resistance, saying "no" to Jesus.

The good news is that it doesn't matter how high, how thick, how tremendous your wall is, Jesus is never deterred. He never gives up. He stands there and knocks. He stands there with open arms and says, "Come to me, *all* who are weary and burdened, and I will give you rest" (Matthew 11: 28).

Who cares if you're on the naughty list, the super-naughty list, or the saccharine-sweet list? What matters is whether you're on the list of those

---

[12] C.S. Lewis said, "Pride leads to every other vice: it is the complete anti-God state of mind…As long as you are proud you cannot know God." *Mere Christianity* (New York: Simon & Schuster, 1943), 110-111.

who've answered the door to Jesus.

When we see the depiction or the reenactment of Jesus lying in the manger over the next few days, may we be reminded that although He was a precious baby two thousand years ago, today He is Precious Lord and Savior of our lives.

Recommended Scripture

Romans 10:5-13

Questions for Reflection

Can you think of a time when Jesus was knocking on the door and you didn't answer? Why didn't you? How can you pray for similar barriers to be overcome by others? How can you share your faith and what it means to you this season?

Closing Prayer

Heavenly Father, thank you for loving me so well. Thank you for pursuing me relentlessly. Thank you for forgiving me for all the years I didn't answer the door. May you move in the hearts of my unbelieving friends, may they come to know You in a real and personal way. May they know in the depths of their souls that they are loved. In Jesus' Name, Amen.

DECEMBER 20
THE FIRST NOËL

Some days are full of good things, really good things, but are draining nonetheless. One December day I had run from one lovely and worthwhile thing to the next from sunrise to sunset. After 9 p.m., I found myself driving my sons home from a swim meet. In the stillness of that dark, cold night *The First Noël* came on the radio. I sat there listening and asking myself what the words meant.

My busy, overloaded mind drew a blank. When I got home I asked my husband, "What does '*The First Noël*' mean?"

He told me that "Noël" is French for Christmas. It is a song about the first Christmas. I wouldn't have blamed him if he had looked at me with wild and shame-filled eyes and said, "What is wrong with you? How could you not know that?" But he didn't. I think he knew I'd had a long day, that I was too tired to think straight, and I appreciated his simple answer and lack of judgment.

I imagine you have days like this too: so full of good things that you wind up too tired for simple recall. Do you too have someone who rightly senses a good time to merely affirm you? Give thanks for them!

Anyway, one stanza of *The First Noël* says:

This star drew nigh to the north-west;
O'er Bethlehem it took it's rest
And there it did both stop and stay,
Right over the place where Jesus lay.

The Magi followed the star so that they could lay their eyes on Jesus. They could only gaze at His face after making a firm commitment and a long journey. But they were determined to see Him.

Today, and every day, not just on Christmas, we can turn our eyes to Jesus without traveling anywhere, without ever having to navigate by a moving star. No matter how busy we've been – just as the old hymn says – "the things of this world will grow strangely dim, in the light of his glory and grace."[13]

Recommended Scripture

Matthew 2:1-12

Questions for Reflection

How can you turn your eyes to Jesus more consistently in the days ahead?

Closing Prayer

Heavenly Father, thank you for sending Jesus. Help me to embrace "the light of His glory and grace" each and every day. In Jesus' Name, Amen.

---

[13] Helen H. Lemmel, *Turn Your Eyes upon Jesus* (1922).

DECEMBER 21
THE DIVINE HELPER

The word "Emmanuel" means "God with us," and during this season of anticipation, we sing with gratitude our reality that Jesus is here! We acknowledge that Jesus knew a humble birth and lived a flawless life, that He died a gruesome death, but rose again three days later. But do we stop to consider how world-altering this was? God walked with Adam and Eve in the Garden, but between the forbidden tree and the tree Jesus died on, there was no Emmanuel. Giants of the faith in the Old Testament knew grace, but even Moses, who encountered God in the burning bush, didn't have the access that we have. Through Jesus, through the physical Emmanuel who walked this earth, we have the indwelling of the Holy Spirit, not some of the time, but all of the time. Remember these words of Jesus?

Nevertheless, I tell you the truth: it is to your advantage that I go away, for if I do not go away, the Helper will not come to you. John 16:7

We have access to the Divine Helper — the Holy Spirit. But do we utilize Him? I hope your honest answer is better than mine, because my honest answer stinks. It's shameful.

Every time I hear the word Emmanuel over the next few days, may it serve as a reminder of how spectacular a reality this little word conveys. Every time I hear it, may I rejoice in my heart that Jesus came as Emmanuel – God with us. And that after He finished His earthly life, He sent us the Holy Spirit, Who is God with us, guiding us into all truth.

Recommended Scripture

John 16:1-15

Questions for Reflection

Can you point to times in your life when you felt the gentle prodding of the Holy Spirit? What happens when you ignore Him? In what specific ways can you more faithfully submit to His guidance and direction?

Closing Prayer

Heavenly Father, please forgive me for all the times that I have pushed aside the prodding of the Holy Spirit. Help me to live each day listening intently and seeking His counsel. Thank you for sending Your Son and for sending Your Spirit. Help me to live my life to Your glory. In Jesus' Name, Amen.

DECEMBER 22
PEACE ON EARTH

When I was a little girl, my grandparents were a major part of Christmas Eve. My mom's three siblings with all their children and our family would gather under one roof. Sometimes we would go to a Christmas Eve service, but regardless of how little or how much church we had sat through, there was absolutely no unwrapping of any gift until Papa had read the Christmas story from Luke 2. That godly man with his kind but firm voice was adamant. We were well-trained and sat in complete silence listening to the stilted language of King James.

We knew that when Papa reached the part about the heavenly hosts proclaiming, "Glory to God in the highest, and on earth peace, good will toward men" we were almost there. It was almost time to tear into those presents like hungry little bears.

I cannot claim to have truly valued this tradition as a child — greedy as I was to open my gifts. Decades later I appreciate how sweet it was. Even now I can hear Papa's voice when I look at the KJV — "it came to pass in those days..."

But why did heavenly hosts proclaim peace? It's not like the two millennia since have been especially peaceful or free from war. Was "peace on earth" just some empty claim that we now sing about with an equal lack of sincerity? Of course not! Peace is the gift that Jesus *offers* — "Peace I leave with you; my peace I give to you," He says in John 14:27. But like any gift, the gift of peace can be discarded, unopened. And sadly, it is readily disregarded, scoffed at, left neatly wrapped, and wholly untried.

One of my favorite little books in the world is Peter Kreeft's *before i go*. It is a collection of very brief essays Mr. Kreeft has written to his grown children — passing on the wisdom he's gained before he goes. This is what he has to say about peace:

> *But unless you are already at peace with yourself, you can't practice the road to peace that is forgiveness. Instead, you will project the war you have with yourself out onto the other. Thomas Merton says we are not at peace with each other because we are not at peace with ourselves, and we are not at peace with ourselves because we are not at peace with God. That's the whole problem of conflict in two sentences.*[14]

Jesus came to offer peace to you, to me, to the world, but not in its collective state. Jesus always deals with the individual. You and I must humbly *accept* His peace. If you stop to think about it, the Bible doesn't record any of examples of Jesus waving His hands over a crowd and pronouncing them all healed. There was a voluntariness to seeking Him out. He met the crowds, preached to the crowds, but healed face to face. And the same is true today, no one can make you accept Jesus – His peace,

---

[14] Peter Kreeft, *Before I go: letters to our children about what really matters* (Lanham: Sheed & Ward, 2007), 124.

purpose, salvation, presence or love. Accepting Jesus is a choice.

Recommended Scripture

John 14:25-31

Questions for Reflection

When do you have the greatest sense of peace? How can you try to know that inner peace more consistently?

Closing Prayer

Heavenly Father, may I live according to Your peace today. May I know that through Jesus I am forgiven for the terrible things I've done in my life, for the people I've hurt, for the people I've ignored, for the good deeds I've left undone. Lord, help me to be a minister of Your peace today. In Jesus' Name, Amen.

DECEMBER 23
COMPASSION FOR A TIRED DONKEY

One of my favorite children's Christmas books is a beautifully illustrated gem called *Room for a Little One*. It tells the Christmas story from the vantage point of animals that took shelter from the cold in the stable before Mary and Joseph arrived. In the book, the animals are hunkered down in the straw when Tired Donkey arrives with Mary on his back. I'm not sure without this book I'd ever contemplate – if Mary did ride on a donkey –whether the donkey was tuckered out by the journey to Bethlehem. But that's the story — that a tired donkey got to be there when the "Little One came for the world."[15]

Do you ever feel like a tired donkey? Because sometimes that's exactly how I feel. One memorable afternoon when my sons were 12, 10 and 6, I felt like all I had done all day was mule them around. I started braying

---

[15] Martin Waddell (Jason Cockcroft, Illustrator), *Room for a Little One: A Christmas Tale*, (Scholastic: New York, 2004).

about it to a friend on the sidelines of a basketball practice I was waiting at, and by the time I was done, I felt I had Eeyored her ear off. Then I felt like a *real* donkey.

My boys had been emotionally draining in various ways — one had had his feelings terribly hurt, one was acting put out over the smallest matters, one accused me of not really trying in a game of Frisbee monkey-in-the-middle. I was frustrated because I definitely could have been doing other things. I could have been washing the dishes in the sink for starters, but instead I was outside playing Frisbee monkey-in-the-middle and was criticized for *effort*!

It wasn't the worst day ever. No one was hurt. There were no tragedies or lasting ill-effects. But don't the small things in life sometimes wear you down? The daily grind in life can be discouraging, and then add to that a crew that is full of complaints and lacking in gratitude, it can turn the sunniest outlook south. And sometimes it's hard to turn the tide because Eeyorism is highly contagious.

But you know what I find really comforting? I find it comforting that Jesus is not a buck-up kind of guy. He doesn't say, "Seriously?!? Are you kidding me? Do you know what I went through for you? You want to know tired? Take a look at Mary in that stable. Take a look at Moses trying to hold his arms up. Take a look at Me on the cross."

No, He doesn't say anything like that. Unbelievably, He says that He will redeem my life from the pit, and crown me with love and compassion (Psalm 103:4). He has *compassion* on a tired donkey like me.

And it doesn't matter what your pit is. You too may have stumbled in with self-pity, or you may have plopped down with the heft of addiction or hopelessness, but no matter how you got there, Jesus is waiting to rescue you, waiting to crown you with love and compassion. How can you not accept an offer like that?

Recommended Scripture

Psalm 103

Questions for Reflection

What kind of pit do you most often find yourself? What does it mean to you to know that Jesus has compassion on you? How can you embrace the redemption that He offers?

Closing Prayer

Heavenly Father, thank you for Jesus, Who is full of compassion and mercy. Thank for redeeming my life from the pit in countless and continuous ways. Thank you that your mercies never end. Help me, Lord, to learn from my mistakes, to listen to the prompting of the Holy Spirit, and to know the depth of Your love. In Jesus' Name, Amen.

DECEMBER 24
THE LIGHT OF THE WORLD

Living in a fallen world means that every day has its sorrows. They never go away. Every day, someone somewhere does something horrific. Every day, hospitals are full of hurting people. Every day, someone loses a child in a car accident. We can relate to the pessimism of Solomon: there *is* nothing new under the sun. This messed up world is reliving the same brokenness over and over again. In some respects, Solomon was dead on: all is vanity, a striving after the wind. But Solomon lived centuries before Christ, and we can agree with his view of the world only so far. We cannot throw our hands up in defeat. Instead, we need to work hard at reconciling our life experiences – that sense of hopelessness – with the truth that Jesus came as The Light of the World. We need to seek out the joy, peace and love of Christ, and to understand that we have a role in His redemptive work.

As the much-loved carol *Joy to the World* says, when He comes again, His blessings will flow as far as the curse is found.

He comes to make His blessings flow
Far as the curse is found,
Far as the curse is found,
Far as, far as, the curse is found.

It is easy for us to see the extent of the curse, and how wonderful to think that when Jesus returns to rule the earth, His blessings will reach just as far. Jesus and His redemption will be everywhere! Yet as we celebrate all that His birth represents for our lives for today and in eternity, we need to think about how we can be ambassadors of His truth and His blessings. A traditional reading on Christmas Eve often contains the following: "He comes! The Light of the world is born this night."

Isn't it interesting that Jesus said that believers are the light of world? In His most famous sermon, the Sermon on the Mount, He said,

You are the light of the world. A city set on a hill cannot be hidden. Nor do people light a lamp and put it under a basket, but on a stand, and it gives light to all in the house. In the same way, let your light shine before others, so that they may see your good works and give glory to your Father who is in heaven. (Matthew 5:14-16)

We are the light of the world. What a privilege and a responsibility. We are called to draw the world to Christ by reflecting Him, to emanate His redemptive light everywhere we go.

As we've counted down the days till Christmas we have looked at many of the promises of the Bible, many of the aspects of God the Father, God the Son, and God the Holy Spirit. As we now turn to celebrating the birth of Jesus with our families and friends, may we live out a fully committed life, acknowledging Jesus as the source of *all* light.

For the past twenty-four days we've made room for the Light. Now may we reflect Him as brightly and clearly as we can -- like a city on a hill!

Merry Christmas!

Recommended Scripture

John 8:12

Questions for Reflection

Do you feel like reading and reflecting daily has helped you make room to celebrate Christmas with deeper meaning? How can you keep reading and reflecting in a systematic way to finish out the Advent season? What devotional or reading plan will you use in the New Year?

Closing Prayer

Heavenly Father, thank you for sending Your Son to earth. Thank you for helping me to draw closer to You. I know, Lord, You are always eager to hear from me, listening to all of my prayers. Help me to continue to spend time with You daily – help me to practice the disciplines of a godly life. Help me to glorify You and reflect Your light wherever I go. In Jesus' Name, Amen.

ABOUT THE AUTHOR

Kristie E. Jackson is an author residing near Chattanooga, Tennessee with her husband and three sons. You can visit her website at www.kristieejackson.com

Made in the USA
Columbia, SC
19 November 2024

47089655R00055